DO YOUR OWN
MOTOR-BIKE
SPRAYING &
CUSTOMIZING

DO YOUR OWN MOTOR-BIKE SPRAYING & CUSTOMIZING

by Paul Revere

W FOULSHAM & CO. LTD

LONDON NEW YORK TORONTO CAPE TOWN SYDNEY

W Foulsham & Company Limited
Yeovil Road, SLOUGH, Berkshire SL1 4JH

ISBN 0–572–01130–X

© Paul Revere 1981

Photoset and printed
in Great Britain by
REDWOOD BURN LTD
Trowbridge & Esher

Contents

1 Introduction

Modern motorcycle manufacturers disagree on just about everything – except one point. Good looks sell motorcycles. To this end they produce carefully styled machines, with bright glistening paintwork and beautiful chrome. But, like everything else that is skin deep, or in this case paintwork deep, its looks will not last forever.

After a couple of years knees wear through the petrol tank paintwork, rubbing cables, salted roads and granite chips take their toll of mudguards, and the occasional spill adds a dent here and a scratch there.

The smart machine that was ridden from the dealers showroom with pride a couple of years earlier, starts to take on the look of a haggard old war horse and its value drops like a stone.

Even fully comprehensive insurance does not help much with the dents and scratches. Most motorcycle policies have an excess clause. This means that the rider pays the first part of any claim and usually for the rider under twenty-five years old, this means paying the first £50. It just so happens that this is about the cost of repairs in a low speed tumble.

1 Removing the petrol cap with gloves on caused these scratches, but they are easily dealt with using do-it-yourself techniques.

2 Some aerosols of paint come complete with emery paper, a small sachet of filler and spreader for really small jobs.

7

3 After you have sprayed your bike a couple of lines on the tank make all the difference. These self-adhesive lines were stuck on in a few minutes.

Below:
4 For thicker lines simply paint between two strips of masking tape. When the tape is removed, a line is left the same thickness as the gap.

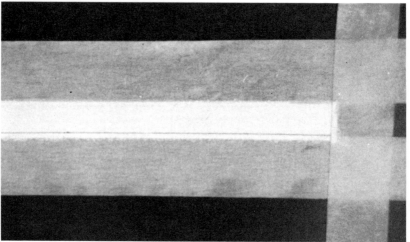

Even the most experienced riders get caught out by loose granite chippings, manhole covers on wet roads, or, even worse, little old ladies who launch themselves into the path of oncoming motorcycles with wild abandon, causing rider and machine to part company through sheer amazement.

The rider can either claim on his insurance, lose a valuable no-claims bonus and find out that the £50 excess covers most of the damage anyway, or keep quiet about it, pay out of his own pocket and spend the next few months avoiding his bank manager.

There is really only one way to keep the bike looking good and still have enough money to buy petrol and that is to do-it-yourself. By using the techniques shown in this book and spending a little time and effort, the average person can successfully tackle jobs from repairing dents and scratches to a complete respray. Instead of paying a high

5 *Power tools save a lot of time. This drill with emery disc will work off the bikes 12V battery.*

6 *Adding accessories can completely transform the appearance of a bike.*

price for a bike in immaculate condition, the rider can also save money be getting the same model with a few dents and scratches considerably cheaper and restoring it.

This is of special interest to the young rider who, because of government legislation, is restricted to motorcycles of 50cc and under at sixteen, but at seventeen can move on to a 250cc machine. On passing the test he or she can then ride a bike of unlimited capacity.

This means that the young rider, in just over a year, will have bought three motorcycles and sold two. Carried out in the normal way, this is a very expensive business and it is not uncommon for a seventeen-year-old to be saddled with considerable hire purchase debts. However, if each bike is bought cheaply and restored using the techniques I describe and then sold at a profit, the transition from moped to big bike can be achieved at little or no cost.

9

2 Materials and Equipment for Repairs

Of all the developments that have helped the do-it-yourself motor-cyclist, the most outstanding has been the development and subsequent improvement of chemical body filler. Filler, as its name implies, is used to fill dents, deep scratches and small holes. It is also used, together with perforated zinc, to fill larger holes and replace rotted sections having a definite shape, such as the edge of mudguards.

It can be bought in various forms. The most complicated and generally most useful type is found in bodywork repair kits containing glass fibre. It comes in three parts – powder, liquid resin and a hardener. This is so that the liquid resin and hardener can be used separately to 'cure' the glass fibre contained in the kit.

1 Most car bodywork repair kits contain glass fibre, resin, hardener, filler powder and bits and pieces to help with mixing and applying.

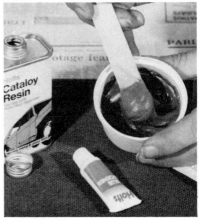

2 Filler powder, resin and hardener are mixed together to form a paste. It should be fairly thick, but still thin enough to hang from a spatula.

The powder is mixed with the liquid resin to form a paste. The consistency of the paste depends on the amount of liquid resin added, and different consistencies of paste have different uses. For example, when filling deep dents on a vertical surface, the filler needs to be fairly thick so that it does not sag, but for smaller dents on a horizontal surface, a thinner paste is preferred. This tends to form a smoother surface when applied and needs less rubbing down.

When hardener is added to this paste, it causes it to set. The hardening action is such that it sets uniformly throughout its thickness and the time taken depends on the amount of hardener added and the temperature. Using more hardener or a higher temperature causes the filler to set quicker, and with less hardener or in colder weather, it takes longer to set. This is an important point to remember because, using the average amount of hardener, filler takes far too long to set in cold weather but on a hot summer's day, it often starts to set before it has been properly worked into the repair. As a general rule, use two-thirds of the normal amount of hardener in summer and one and a half times the normal amount in winter.

The most convenient way to buy filler is as a pre-mix. This usually comes as a tin of ready mixed paste (liquid resin and powder) and a tube of hardener. The paste is of average consistency and the only problem is that on deep dents on vertical surfaces, it has to be applied in layers of about ⅛ inch or less to prevent sagging.

A further refinement of these fillers is a type known as 'elastic'. It is available only as a pre-mix and instead of setting rock hard, it retains some of its flexibility. This makes it less likely to crack when used in areas prone to sudden shock or vibration, but it is slightly less resistant to water than the normal type.

The most common job that filler is used for is to repair a dent. If the dent is deeper than about ¾ inch, when possible, try and reduce its depth by hammering it out from the other side. But be careful – a dent is really a section of stretched metal and if hit too enthusiastically, will turn into a bulge. This, in turn, will have to be knocked back into a dent because you cannot fill a bulge!

Using a medium grade of emery paper (about 200 grade), rub down the area immediately surrounding the dent until you reach bare metal. To help the filler to key in, cut a criss-cross pattern into the dent (but not the surrounding metal) using a screwdriver or the tang of a file.

Next, the filler is mixed. When using the three-part filler for general work, mix the powder and resin to form a fairly stiff paste but not so stiff that, when left for a few moments, the paste will not move to form an even surface. When used on a vertical surface it should be

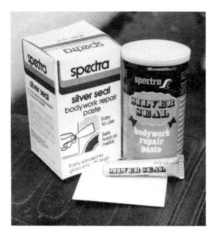

3 When glassfibre is not needed, it is often cheaper and more convenient to buy a pack of hardener and pre-mixed filler paste.

Below:
5 When rubbing down filler on a flat surface, keep the emery paper flat too. Wrap it around a rubbing block.

Above:
4 Filler is used to fill deep dents and scratches. When it has hardened, it is rubbed down to match the surrounding metalwork and sprayed.

6 Before applying filler to a deep dent, the metal surface is scored with the tang of a file or screwdriver to help it key in.

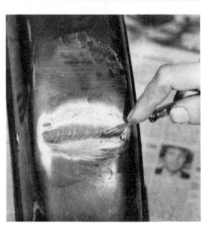

made thicker, but not to the point where it starts to crumble. When mixing powder and resin it is important that it is stirred slowly and thoroughly. If a beating motion is used, pockets of dry powder will be trapped in the paste and when the repair is finally rubbed down, large pinholes will appear.

Next, the hardener is stirred in. Most hardeners have a distinctive colour which is different from the paste and mixing can be seen to be complete when the filler is free from streaks and takes on a uniform colour.

The first layer of filler should be pushed firmly into the dent using a spreader or straight-edged piece of card. Make sure that the first layer has set solidly before applying the next layer and that it is reasonably cool. The chemical action involved in setting generates heat and if filler is applied to a previous layer while it is still warm, it will set far too rapidly.

After the last layer has properly hardened, rub down the filler until it matches the surrounding metalwork, starting with a medium grade of emery paper (about 200 grade) and finishing with a fine grade of about 400. Every so often look along the repair while pouring water over it as this will show up any contour errors. Finally, match the texture of the filler and surrounding metal with a superfine grade of around 600. Wash the area with clean water and dry with a fluff free cloth. When perfectly dry the repair is ready for masking and spraying.

Filler can also be used to repair small holes of around ¼ inch or less. First, using the tang of a file or screwdriver, tap the lip of the hole inwards so that the hole appears like an inverted volcano. Rub down the outer rim of the hole and the area immediately surrounding it with a medium grade of emery paper and push the first application of filler firmly into the hole. The hole should be bridged, but a small indentation will be left in the centre as some of the filler will have been forced through the hole. Apply a second layer, after the first has set, so that the filler is slightly proud of the surrounding area, then rub down in the usual way.

If tiny pinholes appear in a repair, due to insufficient or incorrect mixing of filler, a petroleum-based stopper can be used as further applications of filler are not very effective on tiny holes. Before applying the stopper, clean the repaired area with water and a cloth. When it is completely dry, use a straight-edged piece of card or flexible spreader to wipe a small quantity of stopper across the area containing the pinholes. Press firmly, so that the only stopper left behind is that trapped in the pinholes.

7 Where small pinholes need filling (in this case due to poorly mixed filler) it is often simpler to use a petroleum-based stopper.

Below:
9 Power tools are useful initially for rubbing down large filled areas, but be careful as it is easy to take too much off.

Above:
8 Where a deep scratch has occurred, it can be filled with a filler mix as an alternative to rubbing the whole area down to bare metal.

10 Filler can also be used on holes after they have been bridged from the front or back with glassfibre. This turns the hole into a dent.

Petroleum-based stoppers do not cure like chemical fillers, but rely on the evaporation of the petroleum base into the atmosphere. This means that the surface sets first, so allow about twice this time for the stopper to set through. Otherwise, when the repaired area is sprayed, the petroleum vapour trapped in the stopper will force its way through and cause the paint to blister.

When the stopper has set, rub the area lightly with an extra-fine grade of emery paper, then wash and prepare for spraying.

If a scratch has only penetrated through the paintwork it can be blended in just by using an extra-fine grade of emery paper. However, if the scratch is so deep that metal has been removed, a great deal of rubbing down will be required and there is always the danger that after spraying a slight hollow will be evident.

The simplest way to deal with this type of scratch is to fill it with filler. First, look for any signs of rust in the scratch and if it is evident, treat it with a rust remover. Take care to remove any surplus rust remover with lots of clean water. When dry, mix a small quantity of filler and lay it firmly into the scratch, using a flexible spreader. Always move the spreader at right angles to the scratch so that the scratch acts as a trough and traps the filler. Some fillers appear almost transparent when used in very thin layers, so do not worry if the metal can still be seen. Rub the filler and surrounding paintwork gently with a very fine grade of emery paper until it exactly blends in, then wash and spray.

In motorcycle repairs, glass fibre is used to bridge holes, repair splits, and to reinforce corroded sections. It comes in various thicknesses and textures but generally resembles white fabric and can be cut easily using ordinary household scissors. When impregnated with resin and hardener, it forms a tough skin.

Glass fibre can be divided into three main types, *chopped strand matt, fabric* and *tissue.*

Chopped strand mat gives the greatest strength per layer. It has a very rough texture and is made up of thick strands of glass fibre about 1 inch long. Because of its rough texture and the tendency for its strands to stick out at odd angles, it is of little use to the motorcyclist and is mainly used to reinforce corroded box sections on motorcars.

The most useful type is *glass fibre fabric* which resembles a fine hessian in texture. It is generally used for repairing holes from the back, repairing splits, and reinforcing corroded sections.

The finest type is *glass fibre tissue* and is used almost exclusively for repairing holes from the front. It is virtually a tissue paper made from glass fibre and in its normal state is mechanically very fragile. Great

11 *Glassfibre, impregnated with a resin/hardener mix is used here to reinforce the back of a split tool box cover.*

Below:
13 *As the back of this hole could not be reached, its edges were countersunk and a piece of glassfibre was used to bridge it from the front.*

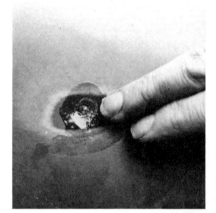

Above:
12 *The normal way to repair a hole is to bridge it from the back with glassfibre tissue impregnated with a resin hardener mix.*

14 *The coarser type of glassfibre is known as chopped strand mat and the finer is called glassfibre tissue. The tissue is most useful for patching small holes.*

care should be taken when impregnating it with resin hardener mix as it can easily disintegrate when wet. Once hardened, it is remarkably strong considering its thickness.

Holes and splits are best repaired from the underside, as this leaves the outside surface flat. Clean the back of the hole or split right down to the bare metal, using a rough grade of emery paper. Place a piece of glass fibre over the back of the hole or split and cut out a patch allowing an overlap of about an inch all round. Where damage is near an edge, do not overlap the edge as the glass fibre will then appear on the outside surface and glass fibre cannot be rubbed down.

Make up a mixture of resin and hardener, lay the glass fibre on a clean surface and using a stippling brush (a stiff short-bristled brush) impregnate the glass fibre with the mixture. The resin hardener mixture is also applied to the back of the metal. The impregnated glass fibre is then held firmly against the metal until it sets. Put a polythene bag over your fingers or they will stick to the metal as well. When the first layer of glass fibre has set, further layers can be added to increase its mechanical strength. When the patch is completely cured, spray the back of the repair with a good quality zinc spray or underseal to prevent future rusting.

On the outside surface, the hole or split is now a very shallow dent and can be filled and rubbed down in the usual manner.

Sometimes it is impossible to get to the back of a hole and it has to be repaired from the front. To do this, the front of the hole is first rubbed down to the bare metal for about an inch all round. Then the tang of a file or a screwdriver is used to countersink the lip of the hole for about half the width of the bare metal. Cut a piece of glass fibre tissue larger than the hole but smaller than the countersunk area and impregnate it with the resin hardener mix. Also apply the resin hardener mix to the countersunk area of the hole and place the piece of glass fibre tissue into position over the hole. When the glass fibre tissue has thoroughly hardened, fill the hole (which is now a dent) with filler and rub down in the normal way.

Where a section has completely rotted away (such as the back of a mudguard) perforated metal is used to replace it. It is usually in the form of zinc or aluminium mesh and can be bought quite cheaply. Most good car bodywork repair kits contain a couple of pieces. Its main job is to act as a base for the filler and, as it is fairly rigid, it can be pre-shaped to match the missing section.

Clean the existing metal back on both sides for a distance of between 1 inch and 3 inches depending on the size of the missing section. Shape a piece of perforated metal to match the missing section and do not forget to allow for the extra 1 to 3 inch overlap on to the previously cleaned metal. Also allow an extra ½ inch on any side of the perforated metal which is to form a new edge. Fold this extra ½ inch back on itself to form a radius edge, but remember that the radius of this edge must be smaller than the edge it is to match up to, otherwise, when filler is applied to the new edge section, it will be too thick.

Prepare a mixture of filler hardener and apply it to the underside of the existing metalwork and that part of the perforated metal that will come into contact with it. Hold the perforated metal firmly in place until it sets, then apply further layers of filler to the perforated metal to build it up to match the missing section. Rub it down until it blends in exactly, then clean and spray.

The only way to really remove rust is to rub the rusted area with emery paper until only bare metal can be seen. Sometimes this is neither advisable or possible. For instance where a scratch has rusted, too much rubbing down may result in a noticeable depression after spraying, or where severe rusting has occurred and the metal has already been well rubbed down but small pits still exist.

In these cases a clear rust remover is used (not a rust removing paint), preferably in the form of a jelly. These rust removers do not actually remove the rust but convert it into a harmless chemical. The rust remover should be applied following the instructions on the container and any surplus thoroughly washed off after it has done its work. Any traces of rust remover which are left can cause problems as they are acidic. Keep rust removers well away from clothing, fingers, and especially eyes.

Cleaning rust from chrome is often a problem. Never use emery paper as this cuts into chrome, ruining its appearance and causing it to rust considerably faster next time. For light surface rust any proprietary brand of chrome cleaner will help, but as most of these are abrasive, constant enthusiastic use will eventually reduce the thickness of the plating and help rusting in the long term.

On suspension units, the use of abrasive chrome cleaners can result in the abrasive getting into the hydraulic seals and reducing the life of the units. One of the safest ways to remove rust from chrome springs on suspension units, wheel rims, and any chromed items not immediately next to paintwork, is by using a nylon pan scrubber and warm soapy water. The nylon is hard enough to remove rust, yet still soft enough not to damage chrome. Unfortunately, it does not do paintwork much good.

When rubbing down filler, wet and dry emery paper should be used. This is a special waterproof paper. Each time it becomes clogged

18

15 *The easiest way to get at rust is to use a nylon, not metal, pan scrubber. Chrome cleaner may get on the hydraulic seals and damage them.*

Below:
17 *This exhaust pipe is well and truly rusted and needs replacing. This is one of the penalties of not cleaning chrome regularly.*

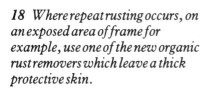

Above:
16 *Where rust has pitted the metal, use a chemical rust remover to neutralise it and then use a filler to smooth over the damaged area.*

18 *Where repeat rusting occurs, on an exposed area of frame for example, use one of the new organic rust removers which leave a thick protective skin.*

19

with filler, it is dipped into water and shaken. The filler embedded in it is released into the water and the paper becomes unclogged.

The texture of the paper is referred to as its grit or grade. An 80 grade is very coarse and should only be used when far too much filler stands proud of a repair. The majority of rubbing down will be done with a medium grade of paper (180 to 220 grade) and the final stages of rubbing down are carried out using a fine grade of around 400. To blend in the texture of a repair before spraying, a superfine paper of about 600 grade is used.

When rubbing down flat surfaces the emery paper should be wrapped around a flat block of cork called a rubbing block. Holding paper in the fingers to rub down a flat surface can produce ridges and hollows.

A quick way to carry out the initial rubbing down of a repair is to use a sanding disc on a power drill. It can also be a quick way to ruin a repair and cut deep grooves in the surrounding metalwork.

The roughest disc to be used should be no rougher than 200 grade. Anything coarser has too fast a cutting rate and is too difficult to control. Wet and dry emery discs are not available because of the obvious dangers of electrocution. Once the disc has run up to speed, wipe it slowly across the filler applying a gentle pressure. Do not stop and start the disc while it is in contact with the filler as this will cause an uneven surface. Also avoid using the edge of the disc as this will cut grooves in the surface.

As each disc begins to clog up, its cutting rate is reduced and there is a natural tendency to press harder. If this pressure is still applied when the disc is changed, the cutting rate will be too high and the drill will either judder and cut grooves in the filler or remove so much filler that the repair goes hollow. Success relies on applying a light steady pressure and keeping the disc moving over the repaired area at a constant speed.

3 Repairing Damage

Dents – *series a*

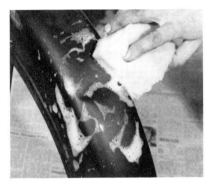

1a It is often easier to take off a mudguard than repair it in place. Before starting, wash the damaged area thoroughly.

2a Using a medium grade of wet and dry emery paper rub the area surrounding the dent down to the bare metal.

3a Periodically wash the damaged area to check progress. When completely rubbed down the area should look like this.

4a Next, using the blade of a screwdriver, scratch the deepest part of the dent to help the filler 'key in'.

5a Wash and rinse thoroughly to remove any traces of loose paint and metal from the dent and surrounding area and dry.

6a Push the filler firmly into the dent to prevent air pockets and use enough to leave it proud of the surrounding paintwork.

Below:
7a When the filler has set hard the initial rubbing down can be carried out with a power tool, but be careful not to take off too much.

8a *The next stage needs to be carried out by hand. It is best to use a rubbing block to level out any humps and hollows.*

9a *This hollow is a fairly common fault and is either caused by using too little filler or by the filler sagging because it is too thin.*

Below:
10a *Another mixture of filler is made up and applied to the hollow. This time make sure to leave it proud.*

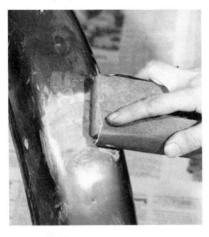

11a *The new filler, when set, is rubbed down to blend with the old. It may appear a slightly different colour as it has not cured for so long.*

12a *As rubbing down proceeds, wash and inspect regularly. The finished repair should match the surrounding area exactly.*

13a *After cleaning, any minor faults such as pinholes, can be filled with a petroleum-based stopper and blended in with superfine emery paper.*

Scratches – *series b*

1b *Deep scratches like this can cause problems. If the scratch has penetrated through to the metal, rusting can occur.*

Below:
3b *Rub down to about half the depth of the paintwork and inspect. In this case rust can be seen in the scratch.*

Above:
2b *First, rub down the surrounding area. This will remove any surface irregularities caused by the scratch.*

4b *A liquid rust remover is used to neutralise the rust in the scratch. Keep the rust remover away from fingers and clothes.*

5b *Allow a few minutes for the rust remover to work. Different makes take different times. Then wash thoroughly.*

Below:
7b *Using a superfine grade of emery paper, rub the filler down gently until the repair matches the surrounding paintwork.*

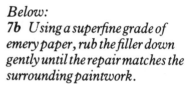

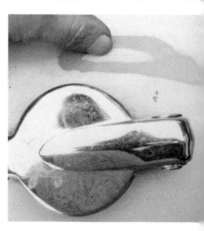

Above:
6b *When the scratch is perfectly dry, push a little filler/hardener mix into it, making sure it stands proud of the surrounding paintwork.*

8b *The finished repair will have a fine line of filler in place of the scratch. Check with a thumb nail that the surface is smooth.*

9b Scratches which only penetrate a layer or two of paint are easily dealt with as rust will not be present.

10b Rub down the paintwork surrounding the scratch with superfine emery paper. Wash and inspect frequently.

11b When the layer of paint that the scratch has reached is rubbed down, the scratch will disappear completely.

Holes – *series c*

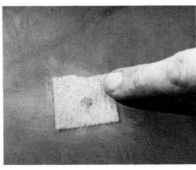

Above:
1c *When it is possible to reach the back of a hole, both sides should first be thoroughly cleaned with fine emery paper.*

2c *Cut a piece of glassfibre tissue considerably larger than the hole and impregnate it with resin/hardener mix.*

3c *Also apply a resin hardener mix to the back of the hole. It should cover a greater area than the size of the piece of glassfibre.*

Above:
4c Stick the piece of impregnated glassfibre firmly in position over the back of the hole. Avoid air bubbles being trapped.

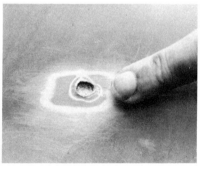

5c From the front, the hole is now virtually a dent. The glassfibre bridging it forms the bottom of the dent.

6c When the glassfibre has set, the hole is filled with a filler mix, then rubbed down in the usual way.

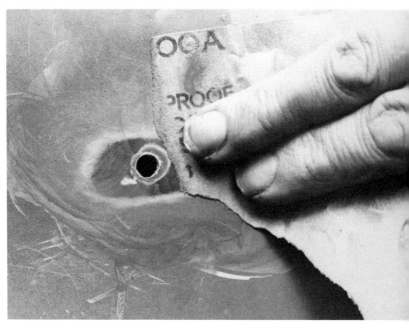

Above:
7c When it is not possible to get at the back of a hole, start by rubbing down the front of the hole with emery paper.

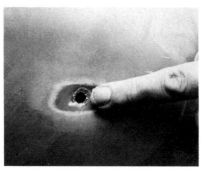

8c Next, the area around the edge of the hole is knocked inwards from the front using the blade of a screwdriver.

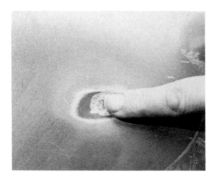

9c A piece of glassfibre tissue is cu so that it is bigger than the hole but smaller than the knocked-in area.

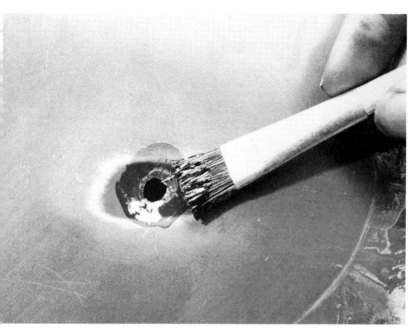

Above:
10c The area around the hole is brushed with resin/hardener mixture. Do not apply too much as it may run.

11c The piece of glassfibre is also impregnated with the resin/hardener mix and pushed firmly into place over the hole.

12c The hole is now bridged and when the glassfibre has set, it can be filled and rubbed down in the usual way.

Rust – *series d*

1d *This rather nasty patch of rust occurred because a loose control cable had rubbed away the paintwork.*

2d *Wash and rub down gently with fine wet and dry emery paper until bright metal just starts to appear.*

3d *As can be seen, pits of rust have eaten deep into the metal. More rubbing down would result in a hollow.*

4d *Rust remover is applied to neutralise the pits of rust. As the pitting was deep, two applications were required.*

5d *After the second application had been given plenty of time to work, it was washed off with lots of water and thoroughly dried.*

6d *Filler was then applied and pushed firmly into the affected area to avoid air bubbles forming.*

7d *Blend the filler in with fine emery paper. It does not matter if metal shows through as long as its surface is smooth.*

Below left:
8d *Usually, the first sign that rust is attacking paintwork is the appearance of these small pinholes.*

Below right:
9d *At this stage the rust will not have penetrated the metal, so a quick rub with fine emery paper is all that is needed.*

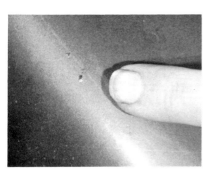

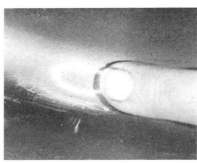

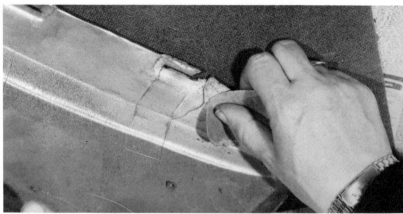

Splits – *series e*

Opposite top:
*1e Plastic covers are easily split
and expensive to replace.
Repairing with glassfibre and filler
is fairly easy.*

Opposite centre:
*2e Clean both sides of the damaged
area. Roughen up the inside with
emery paper for about 3 inches
either side of the split.*

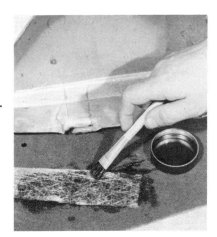

Opposite bottom:
*3e Cut a piece of glassfibre to cover
the roughened area, and match its
shape to the edge of the item being
repaired.*

Top:
*4e Impregnate the glassfibre with
a mixture of resin and hardener
until it is thoroughly soaked
through.*

Centre:
*5e Apply the resin/hardener mix to
cover an area slightly larger than
will be covered by the glassfibre.*

Bottom:
*6e Lay the glassfibre on to the
repair and press down firmly. Make
sure that no air bubbles are trapped.*

35

7e When the repair has thoroughly hardened, use a sharp knife to remove any glassfibre or resin around the hinge hole.

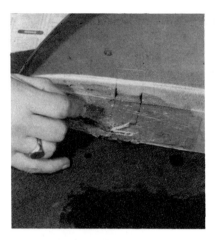

8e Filler is now applied to the outside to fill in any gap left by the split. The filler should stand slightly proud.

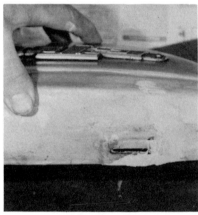

Below:
9e When set the filler is rubbed down. Pop a piece of card in any holes to avoid enlarging them.

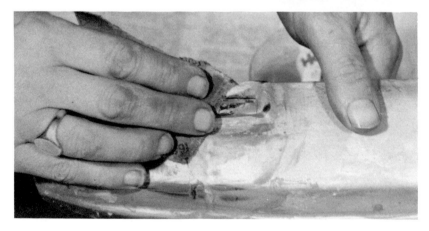

4 Materials and Equipment for Spraying

If you point a spray gun at an object and pull the trigger, it will do two things. It will spray where you want it to *and* where you do not want it to. This is because the paint coming out of the gun is in the form of different-sized particles, propelled by a stream of air.

By the time these particles have travelled the 8 to 10 inches from gun to object, the larger particles have spread out to an area of about 6 inches and the smaller ones, which can be deflected easily by the smallest breeze, often miss their target by a foot or so.

If you think of it in terms of trying to paint something with a paint brush about a foot wide, it is easy to see why the paint seems to go everywhere except where it is intended. A little spray 'drift' landing on chrome is no problem because it can easily be removed with thinners but when it gets on to clear plastic items, like a speedometer lens, life can get a little difficult. Use thinners on clear plastic items and the chances are that they will turn milky. Try and scrape it off and the plastic gets scratched. The answer is not to let it get there in the first place. This is the reason for masking off areas that are not to be sprayed. The two most useful materials for this job are masking tape and old newspapers, with petroleum jelly making a valuable but tricky-to-use third.

Masking tape is a special kind of sticky tape. It has an adhesive surface that sticks well to metal and paintwork, but not so firmly as to pull the paintwork off when it is removed. It is easy to tear off to length and has a paper-like backing. It is stuck to plastic and chrome items to protect them from spray drift and used to hold newspapers in place to protect larger areas.

The tape copes well with paint but problems can occur if it gets wet. With the cheaper tapes, the paper-like backing loses its strength and comes away in strips. This leaves the adhesive still firmly in place and it does not seem to respond to any safe solvents. The only way to remove it is to scrape it off, with the obvious danger of scratching the surface it is stuck to. The best insurance against this happening is to use only well-known brands of tape.

Petroleum jelly (ie, Vaseline) can be applied sparingly to small items which are hard to get at and impossible to mask with tape. When the petroleum jelly is wiped off the unwanted paint comes off with it. Hands should always be washed thoroughly after applying petroleum jelly, as one greasy fingermark on a petrol tank or mudguard before it is sprayed will mean that the whole job will have to be done again. To add insult to injury, it only becomes apparent when the paintwork is polished, and a piece of paint the size of the fingermark suddenly comes adrift. If a piece of jelly accidentally comes into contact with an area about to be sprayed, wiping it off with a rag just makes it worse. Because it cannot be seen does not mean that it is not there, just that it has been spread over a greater area. A good wash with soap and warm water or, better still, white spirit is what is needed.

Spray guns come in all sorts of shapes, sizes and prices, but they all rely on the fact that a stream of paint mixed with a fast-moving stream of air turns into a stream of fine particles of paint. This is the spray that comes out of the end of the gun.

There are two main ways to achieve this: either mix the paint with a lot of low pressure air or a little high pressure air.

Low pressure guns are usually easy to recognise. They are inexpensive, work off mains electricity and have a small compressor built into the handle. This vibrates when the gun is switched on and supplies the air.

High pressure units are expensive. They are the type normally used by garages and have a separate compressor and air tank. They are the best type of gun for spraying motorcycles for many reasons. First, they are easier to use. They also spray a greater volume of paint per second, and the thickness of the paint (ratio of paint to thinners) is not so critical. Using this type of unit, even the thickest type of metalflake can be sprayed. Unfortunately, even the cheapest will cost about the same as three good tyres and the more expensive units will cost more than a good second-hand bike. Buying a unit of this type would only be worth considering if more than one bike was being resprayed.

For the do-it-yourself man or woman there is a way to get all the advantages of a high pressure unit at a fraction of the cost – by using aerosols. An aerosol of paint is basically a high pressure spray gun. The can contains the paint and its own supply of high pressure propellant (usually an inert gas so that the paint will not deteriorate during storage). The mixing takes place, in exactly the correct proportions, in the nozzle.

Colour matching presents no problems either, as each aerosol has a code stamped on its base, related to the colour of paint it contains. The accessory dealer uses this code and a chart supplied by the aerosol manufacturer, together with the paint code on the bike to get an exact match. As an extra safeguard, the manufacturers spray the lids of the aerosols with a sample of the paint contained in it. This means that if the paint code has been obscured or if there is reason to suspect that the bike has been resprayed by a previous owner, the paint on the lid can be compared to the bike's paintwork outside the accessory shop and any problems sorted out there and then.

If the bike is being completelely resprayed and it is not intended to use the manufacturer's original colour, racks of aerosol paints can be a source of inspiration. The racks in a major accessory shop will contain just about every colour available for two or four-wheeled vehicles. Why not use a car colour or a metallic finish? Make a note of the number on the bottom of the can and keep it somewhere safe, so that next time you buy an aerosol to touch up a scratch or dent, it is the new colour and not the old one.

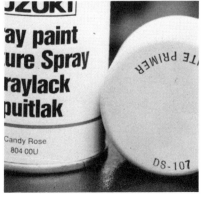

1 Most aerosols have samples of their colours sprayed on to their lids. If possible check the lid with your bike before buying.

2 Manufacturers stamp reference numbers on their aerosols. Once you get a match, make a note of the number.

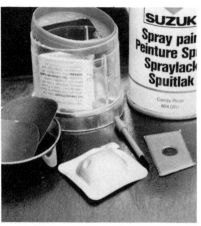

3 Some aerosols have 'extras' in the lid. This one contains stopper, a spreader, emery paper and a touch-up brush.

Below:
5 To use a brush with aerosols, spray a little paint into the lid. After a few seconds, it will be thick enough to use.

Above:
4 Masking tape comes in different widths. The narrowest is used for masking small items, and the widest is used for sticking down newspaper.

6 These little 'chips' are very difficult to tackle with an aerosol. A little paint on a touch-up brush is easier.

5 The Technique of Masking

The purpose of masking is to prevent paint from going where you do not want it to go. It sounds easy, but before you pick up your roll of masking tape and bundle of old newspapers, make sure that the area about to be sprayed is clean and smooth and free from dust, polish or anything else that might prevent the paint from sticking to it. Once the masking is in place, that quick last rub down and wash will ruin the tape and paper and the whole job will have to be done again.

Assuming that all is well, the next step is to decide in detail how the job is to be tackled. Always be thorough. Miss a small gap and the spray that creeps through could be a problem to remove; but do not go to the other extreme and mask for the sheer hell of it. Try to be as efficient as possible.

If it is intended to completely respray a front mudguard, and the mudguard is left on the bike, a great deal of masking will be necessary. First, the front wheel will have to be covered over with newspapers. Then the forks will need to be wrapped in newspaper and bound with masking tape to keep the paper in place. The front of the frame, engine and exhaust manifolds will also need to be protected from spray drift and any cables in the way will either have to be disconnected or bound with tape. Alternatively, most mudguards can be removed by undoing four nuts. It can then be placed upright on a couple of sheets of newspaper (so that you do not spray the road) and you are ready to go.

Instruments that are sunk into headlamp cowlings are often difficult to mask. The simplest way is to lay the end of the masking tape on to the instrument glass so that its outer edge just meets the paintwork on the cowling. Follow the glass around until the tape forms a complete circle. Next cut a piece of newspaper so that it covers the exposed glass and half the width of the tape. Apply another layer of tape over the first, so that half the width of the tape sticks to the paper and half to the previous layer of tape. The instrument is now paint-proof.

Petrol filler caps are another source of trouble. Basically there are two kinds, the twist off and the hinged lockable. The twist off cap is easily removed by simply twisting it off, but it leaves a hole. Spraying paint into a petrol tank is a quick way to clog up filters and carburettor jets, so the hole must be masked.

When the cap is removed and the hole examined (cigarettes OUT), an unpainted rim around the hole will be seen. Clean and dry this rim as any petrol on it will affect the adhesive properties of the tape. Then lay the end of the tape on so that its outer edge covers the unpainted rim and butts up to the paintwork. Run the tape around the hole until it forms a circle. Do not try and push paper into the hole to block it because it will probably fall into the tank. Instead, use strips of tape, bridging them across the previously formed tape circle. Do not let them protrude beyond the edge of the tape circle as they will then mask off the paintwork around the hole.

Hinged filler caps are far easier to deal with. These are simply bound with tape from where the cap meets the base upwards until the flat top is reached. The top is masked by sticking strips of tape across it. If the cap is of the lockable type take special care to mask the keyhole properly, otherwise the lock will jam.

Rear shock absorbers with their springs exposed are a trap for the unwary. They are easily masked, using a piece of paper wrapped around them to form a tube. Masking tape is used to hold the tube together and in place on the shock absorber body. Try and bind the springs with masking tape and the tape slips between the coils of the springs and gets stuck to itself. There are more exciting things to do with life than fishing out bits of masking tape from coil springs with a bent hat pin!

1 Cut masking down to the minimum by removing bits and pieces where possible. Two screws remove this lettering.

2 To mask a repaired area, form a square of tape around it leaving a few inches of clear space either side.

Below:
4 Stick the other half of the tape to that already in place. Seal gaps between the sheets of newspaper with more tape.

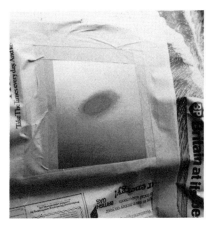

Above:
3 Attach strips of wide tape to newspaper, so that half of the tape's width is stuck to the paper and half is free.

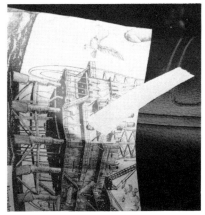

5 Stick the free edges of the paper down so that they are not blown on to the repair during spraying.

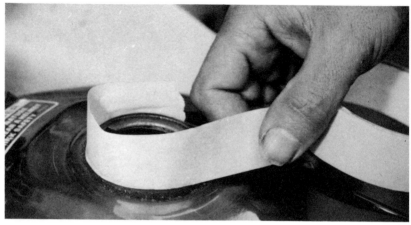

Above:
6 *Petrol filler caps can be difficult. Remove the detachable type and place a ring of masking tape around the hole.*

7 *Push the tape inwards to help it stick to the edge of the hole. This is used next to attach more tape.*

8 *Stick strips of tape across the gap and stick to the already formed tape ring. Do not let them go past the ring or the tank will be masked.*

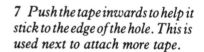

9 *Hinged top filler caps often have high necks. Do not mask the neck as it will be seen when the cap is closed.*

Below:
10 *With the cap closed, mask around its edge. Let the tape overlap underneath, but make sure it does not mask the neck.*

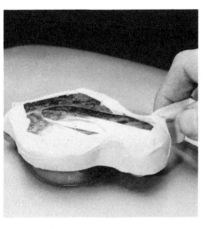

Above:
11 *Pass a loop of tape around the hinge and lock to prevent paint getting in and causing them to stick.*

12 *Cover the top with overlapping strips of tape. Do not bring them down the sides or they will mask the neck.*

45

13 *It is difficult to get paint off numberplates. First, cut out a piece of paper slightly smaller than the numberplate.*

14 *Apply wide masking tape so that about one-third sticks to the paper, one-third to the numberplate and the rest overlaps under the edge.*

46

6 The Technique of Spraying

The idea behind spraying is fairly simple – to apply even coats of paint to the bike. But in practice it can get complicated, so start with the basic material – paint.

Remember that the paintwork on a bike consists of two basic coats, the primer and top coat. The primer is the first coat to be applied and always has a matt finish. It is a special type of paint, formulated to adhere well to metal. Its matt surface also provides a good base for the top coat to key into.

Some years ago there were only two colours of primer in general use, red (usually referred to as red lead or red oxide) and grey. Since the introduction of exotic bike colours by manufacturers, the number of primer colours has increased considerably. This is because the colour of the primer has some effect on the shade of the final coat. Although this is more noticeable on the lighter colours, the mid-range colours can be affected as well. For example, a middle to light red sprayed over a white primer gives a really bright red finish. Yet the same red sprayed over a dark red primer gives a finish nearer maroon.

If the whole bike is being sprayed and an exact match is not needed, the matching of primers can be ignored, but if a repair or part of a bike is being sprayed, then it is essential that primers are matched as far as possible.

During preparation it was probably necessary, somewhere on the bike, to rub the paintwork down to the bare metal. Where this occurred, a ring of paint surrounding the bare metal will have appeared. This ring is the colour of the primer. If the paintwork has not been rubbed down this far, use a piece of superfine emery paper and rub a small section of paintwork in an area to be resprayed until the primer appears.

Respraying can be carried out so well that you might have bought a resprayed bike and not know it. If it has been resprayed to match the manufacturer's original colour, there are no problems but if the colour has been changed you could end up accidentally buying the wrong colour of paint. If there is any doubt, take a small chip of paint

1 If the top coat is applied to the primer before the primer is properly dry, this 'shattered surface' effect can occur.

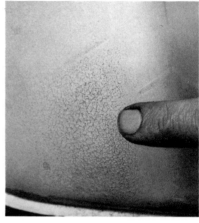

Below:
2 Always keep the aerosol at right angles to the surface being sprayed and at the distance stated by the manufacturer.

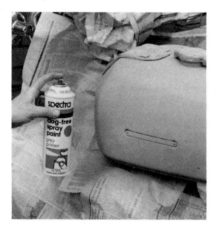

Above:
3 Never forget to spray the under edges of objects with both primer and top coat or flaking may occur later.

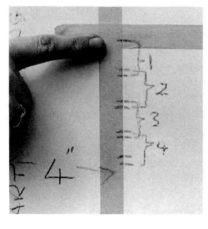

4 This paper is masked and marked for practice. The numbered marks show the width of the spray for the first few strokes.

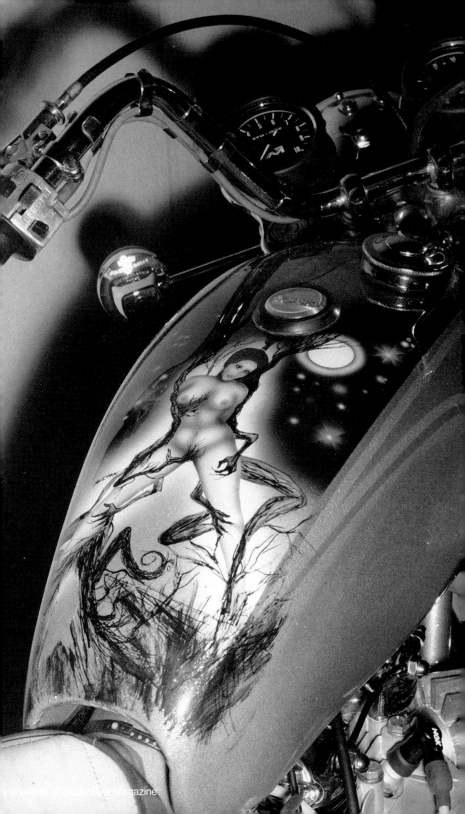

or, better still, the bike itself down to your local accessory dealer and check the colour against the top of the aerosol before you buy. There may be a slight difference because of the ageing of the paintwork, but any marked difference and you have got the wrong can. The only thing to do in a situation like this is to go through the whole range of aerosols in that particular colour until you get a match.

If you are using a spay gun and buying paint by the pint, the problem is slightly more complicated because you will probably have to choose paint from a colour card and mix two together to get an exact match. This is quite a tricky business and is yet another argument for using aerosols.

If possible, practise spraying on a large piece of newspaper or card. Ideally, it should be about the size of a petrol tank, so that the finish can be checked for various faults that are associated with the sweeping action required to cover an area this size. When spraying your practice piece remember the following:

1 Always keep the aerosol can or spray gun level with the surface you are spraying, so that the sprayed paint comes out at right angles to the surface being sprayed.
2 Never hold the aerosol or gun still while it is still spraying.
3 Move the aerosol or gun at a constant speed over the surface to be sprayed at about 1½ to 2 feet per second.
4 Release the trigger or button at the end of each stroke *before* the gun stops moving.
5 Hold the gun or aerosol the correct distance from the surface, as specified by the manufacturers. The correct distance for one kind of gun may not be the correct distance for another.

When spraying, it usually helps to think of the sprayed paint as a wide band of delicate self-adhesive colour which is being laid on to the object.

When you are ready to spray the bike, make sure that the weather is suitable. If it is too damp, the finish will be dull because the paint picks up moisture from the air. This dullness is not just on the surface and cannot be removed with cutting compounds. It goes all the way through.

Spraying on a hot sunny day also causes problems. The metal of the bike heats up and causes the paint to dry almost on impact, giving a very rough finish to the surface. If it is necessary to spray on a day like this, move the bike into the shade well beforehand, to give it plenty of time to cool down.

When atomised paint leaves the gun, it is very light and can easily be blown off course by anything stronger than a very light breeze. The normal reaction to this is to hold the spray nearer, which results in uneven coverage and paint runs. It also means that any vehicles parked too near will also get sprayed! So wait until the wind dies down.

Start at the top left-hand corner of the area to be sprayed. Move the aerosol so that it is positioned slightly before the starting point. This is to give sufficient distance to start the aerosol moving at the correct speed before the spray button is pressed. Spray with a clean sweep across the area and stop spraying at the end, but keep the gun moving. Check where the paint actually went and repeat slightly lower, so that the bands of paint overlap without leaving any trace of a gap or unevenness. Continue moving down until the area is completely covered.

Technique Practice – *series a*

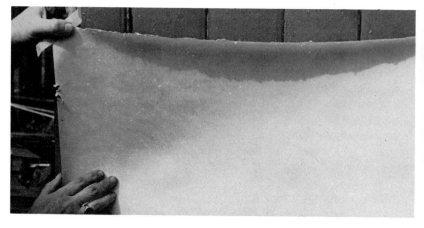

1a The quickest way to learn to spray is to fasten up a large piece of paper. Newspaper will do but cartridge paper shows up faults better.

2a Using normal masking tape, mark out an imaginary panel, but do not mask off the surrounding area with newspaper.

3a Remember that if this was a real item, the only area to receive the spray would be inside the masking tape.

Below:
4a About 4 inches either side of the masking tape, mark out two lines. Mark the first 'start spraying' and the second 'stop spraying'.

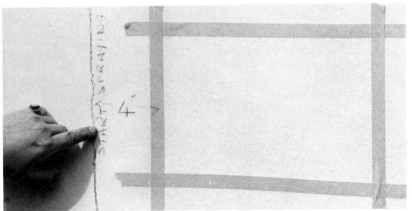

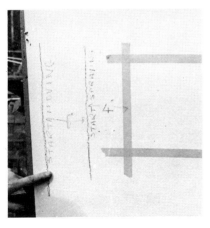

5a A further 6 inches either side of these lines, mark out another pair. Mark the first 'start moving' and the second 'stop moving'.

6a *When spraying, the can is held in the 'start moving' position, and from there it is moved across to be sprayed at a constant speed.*

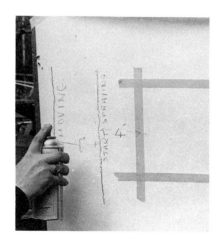

7a *When the aerosol passes the 'start spraying' line, the button is pressed and held down. Remember to keep the aerosol moving.*

Below:
8a *Keep the aerosol moving at a constant speed and distance away from the object. On passing the 'stop spraying' line, the button is released.*

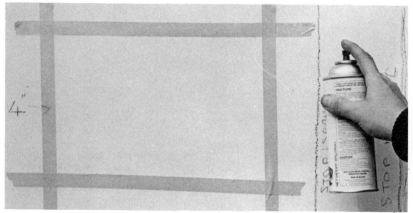

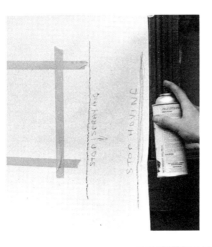

9a *Do not stop moving the aerosol as soon as the button is released, but keep it moving a little longer (in this case, to the 'stop moving' line).*

Below:
10a *Holding the aerosol at the correct distance make one spray line. Draw a line on either side of the solid part and this is its effective width.*

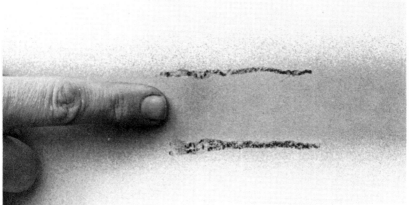

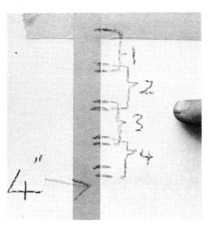

11a *Transfer this width to the next masked area. Allowing for an overlap on each spray line, mark out the first few spray lines as shown.*

12a Using this method, spraying can be quickly mastered. Remember, the only spraying that counts is that in the masked area.

Below:
13a Running paint is one of the most serious faults and is caused either by holding the aerosol too close or moving it too slowly.

Above:
14a Holding the aerosol too far away results in the paint partially drying and forming into small rough blobs.

15a Bands appear if the can is brought down too much after each stroke. To put right, spray over in the correct way.

When spraying, the following faults may occur:

1 Paint runs. These are ridges of paint that have sagged down or, at worst, drops of running paint. This is the result of putting on too much wet paint at once and can be caused by holding the gun or aerosol too close or not moving it along fast enough. If the fault appears at the left-hand edge only, the spray button was pressed before the aerosol had started moving and if at the right-hand edge, the aerosol was stopped before the button was released.

2 Orange peel. This fault gets its name from its surface, which is like orange peel, and is usually caused by holding the spray too close to the surface. The paint does not sag or turn into runs as the aerosol is invariably moved along too fast as well.

3 Rough finish. When the aerosol or spray is held too far from the surface, the smaller droplets of paint start to dry before they reach it. Consequently, these small 'pieces' of paint cannot flow to form a smooth surface. This can easily be corrected by rubbing with an abrasive polish or cutting compound.

4 Spitting. This is a fault with the aerosol or spray gun. In the case of a gun it is usually caused by incorrect adjustment of the nozzle or the wrong ratio of paint to thinners. Insufficient mixing of the paint and thinners can also cause this problem.

In the case of an aerosol, it is usually because the can has had insufficient shaking before use or a drip has formed on the spray nozzle. This can easily be removed with a paper handkerchief or piece of kitchen roll. Do not use woolly rags because small hairs may stick to the nozzle and cause further problems.

5 Colour variations. Again this is the result of failing to shake the aerosol can properly, or in the case of a spray gun, insufficient mixing of the paint.

6 Bands. When a resprayed section is viewed from an angle, sometimes bands of tonal variation can be seen. This is because the aerosol or spray gun has been moved too far down after each stroke. Although there is no obvious gap between each stroke (because the edge of the spray pattern has just managed to cover it) the coating in this area is extremely thin. This gives the impression of bands of varying tone. The solution is to wait until the paint is dry and then apply another coat, taking care not to make the same mistake again.

Once the first coat of primer has dried, the quality of the preparation will become obvious. Any minor scratches or blemishes can easily be seen and should be dealt with before going any further. If you leave them and hope they will disappear when the job is finished and then find out they have not you will have to start all over again.

At least two coats of primer should be used and where the paintwork has been rubbed down to the bare metal, preferably three. After the last coat of primer has dried, perfectionists say that it should be gently rubbed down with superfine emery paper, preferably lubricated with a little soap (not detergent). In practice, this is a matter of choice. If the surface feels rather rough it could be that at times the spray was held too far away, or the surface being sprayed was rather warm. Under these circumstances, it is worth using the 'emery and soap' treatment, but it should be carried out carefully as the emery paper cuts away the uppermost layer of the primer. Rub too hard and you could end up with bare metal again.

If careful inspection shows that the coats of primer are completely smooth and free from blemishes, the first coat of colour or 'top coat' can be applied.

Again, at least two and preferably three coats of colour should be used, and each coat should be thoroughly dry before the next is applied. It is worth remembering at this stage that it is the paint that stops the bike rusting and therefore the more coats of paint applied, within reason, the longer the finish will last. Some brands of car polish contain an abrasive (who makes bike polish?). The abrasive acts as a cutting agent and removes a fine film of paint every time the polish is used. It is very effective in returning the sparkle to faded paintwork, but if used too often and too vigorously, it is equally effective in removing the paintwork! So a combination of too thin a layer of colour and over-enthusiastic polishing could result in the primer showing through in less than a year.

Before removing the masking, make sure that not only has the paint on the bike dried but the paint on the masking is dry too. The easiest way to check this is to locate any small runs on the masking tape and see if they have hardened all the way through. As a rule of thumb, with aerosols, allow about 40 minutes on a reasonably warm day. In colder weather, or when using a spray gun it could take up to an hour.

As soon as the masking is removed, the new paintwork can be examined. The most usual faults are small areas which have been left unsprayed, due to overmasking, and take the form of fine lines around chromework, etc.

Tins of 'touch up paint' are ideal for dealing with this kind of problem. Each tin comes complete with its own small brush built into the lid (though some kinds of aerosol have this facility). The tin should always be shaken for about two minutes before use and the lid/

brush removed and allowed to drain for a few seconds. Drips of paint remaining on the brush should be gently wiped off on to the inside neck of the tin. The paint is then applied lightly with the tip of the brush. As a paint run at this stage would result in a great deal of work, it is safer to apply a few light coats than one heavy one.

If paint runs are present, allow at least 24 hours for the paint to harden, then rub the runs gently with a piece of superfine emery paper until they blend in with the surrounding paintwork. Wipe away any resulting paint powder with a cloth and 'blow' over the immediate area with an aerosol of colour to blend in the surface texture.

Areas suffering from orange peel and roughness can also be salvaged by rubbing down with superfine emery paper and then being given a light coat of colour.

About a week after respraying, the final treatment can be given, which gives the paintwork its deep gloss. First, using a cutting compound (the liquid kind is preferred) and a soft cloth, gently rub the paintwork until a gloss starts to appear, then wash the paintwork and change to a mildly abrasive polish. These polishes are usually called 'colour restorers' and should be used sparingly until a deep gloss is obtained.

Next, wash the whole area and when bone dry, polish with a reputable brand of wax polish.

Sometimes a really deep plate-glass finish is required. This is normally wanted by people who 'customize' their bikes and it looks really startling over metal flake. There is no good reason why this kind of finish should not be applied to a bike in ordinary manufacturer's colours, but it does require a fair amount of extra work.

When the paintwork has reached the stage where it is ready for waxing, do not wax it. Instead re-mask it for spraying. The idea is to spray the paintwork with layers of clear lacquer, but before actually spraying, make sure that paint and lacquer are compatible.

This is easily done by spraying any piece of metal (even a baked bean can) with paint, then when it is dry spray it with lacquer. If nothing strange happens, spray the bike's paintwork with three or four layers of lacquer in the usual way (as if using paint), but *do not* rub down with emery paper or even abrasive polish as this will ruin the super gloss. Leave for about a week (so that the lacquer is glass hard), then apply a good quality wax polish with a soft cloth.

Spraying Repaired Areas – *series b*

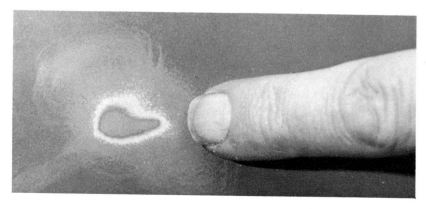

Above:
1b First make sure that the area to be sprayed is clean and dry. Any dampness or grease will affect the finished paintwork.

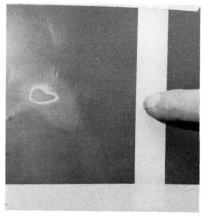

2b Start masking by forming a square of masking tape around the repaired area. Leave a clear area of about 3 inches all around if possible.

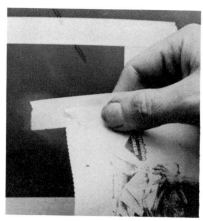

3b Apply masking tape to pieces of paper so that half the width of the masking tape is stuck to the paper and half is left free.

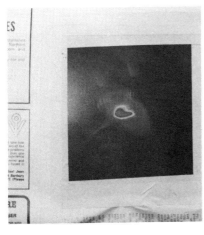

4b *Stick the paper in position so that the free half of the masking tape sticks to the tape already in position.*

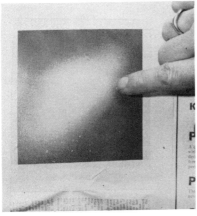

5b *Apply primer and top coat carefully, so that they do not go to the edge of the tape. A little spray drift to the edge of the tape does not matter.*

Below:
6b *When the paint has thoroughly hardened, blend it in using a mildly abrasive polish. Small ledges caused by spray drift will then disappear.*

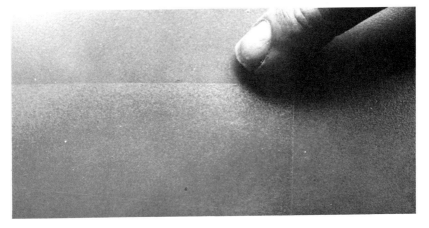

Spraying a Petrol Tank
– series c

1c *The first step is to put right any damage. This light scratch can easily be removed with a small piece of fine emery paper.*

Below:
2c *After it has been rubbed down, clean thoroughly with water, so that the repair can be checked properly.*

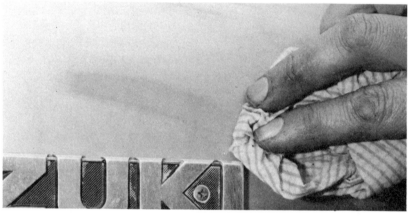

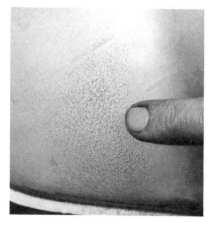

3c *This area of shattered paint will have to be thoroughly rubbed down until it is glass smooth or it will show on the finished paintwork.*

4c On this particular bike the tank lettering is easily removed. If it cannot be, either mask it or rub it down and re-letter later.

Below:
5c Rust often appears under the lip of the tank. Rub down and use a rust remover if pitting is present.

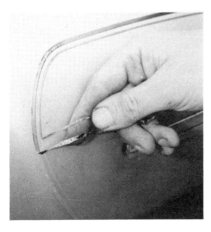

6c Rub down any lining as it is impossible to mask. This lining was 'stick on' and had to be carefully peeled off.

61

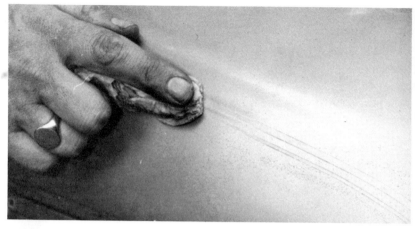

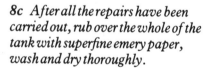

Above:
7c 'Stick-on' lining leaves a sticky residue which has to be removed with a solvent. Do not and the paint will not stick properly.

8c After all the repairs have been carried out, rub over the whole of the tank with superfine emery paper, wash and dry thoroughly.

9c The next step is masking. Remember to take special care when masking locks on petrol tanks, etc. If paint gets into them they may jam.

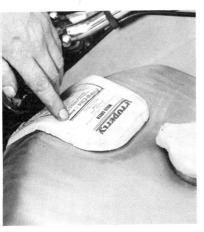

10c *It is often easier to mask off different coloured small sections of the tank, than to have to respray them later.*

11c *Releasing the dual seat and releasing the rear of the tank only takes a couple of minutes and makes masking a great deal easier.*

Below:
12c *Lift the tank slightly and slide under sheets of paper so that they are held in place by the frame. They should not touch the underside of the tank.*

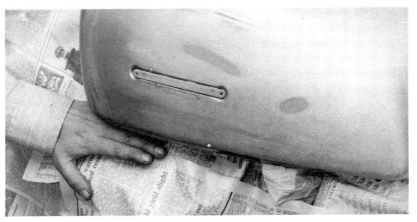

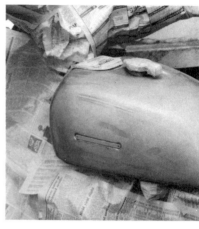

13c Wrap the handlebars with newspaper and tape and extend the masking as far as possible. Join the edges of the paper together with more tape.

14c Apply at least two coats of primer. Wait until each coat has dried before applying the next, and do not forget the underside of the tank.

15c At this stage rub down any paint blemishes in the primer with superfine emery paper. It is easier than doing it when the top coat has been applied.

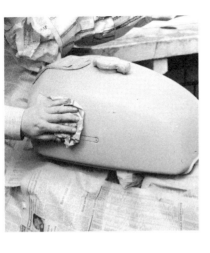

16c Wipe away any rubbed down primer dust with a damp (not dripping wet) fluff-free cloth and allow to dry.

17c Next, apply at least two coats of colour. As the second coat of colour is applied, a gloss surface should appear.

Below:
18c Wait until the paint is completely dry before removing the masking. Paper or tape coming into contact with a sticky paint surface could cause considerable damage.

Below right:
19c Wait a few days until the paint has fully hardened and bring to a glass-like surface using a mildly abrasive polish.

Spraying Ancillary Items
— series d

1d It is easier to spray oil feed tanks on the bike as removal could cause problems with air locks in the oil feed system.

2d Removing the dual seat is worthwhile. It is a simple job and gives better access to the top of the oil tank.

3d If possible remove any lettering, etc. If it cannot be removed or masked it will have to be rubbed down and replaced later.

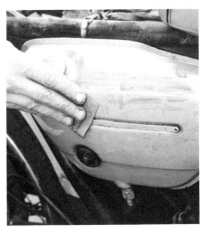

4d *Rub down the surface of the oil tank with superfine wet and dry emery (do not forget the edges), then wash and dry thoroughly.*

5d *Before masking the oil filler hole, clean it thoroughly. Masking tape will not adhere to an oily surface.*

6d *The plastic oil level window will be difficult to remove paint from, so mask it with a ring of tape.*

7d *When the ring of tape is pushed inwards, it forms an effective mask. Do not let it stick out and mask the tank.*

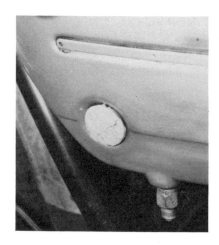

8d *The tank can be masked by pushing newspaper behind it. Make sure the pieces of paper overlap well, or spray will get through.*

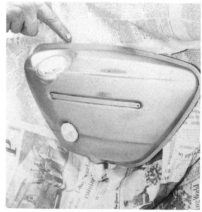

Below:
9d *Spray in the usual way with at least two coats each of primer and colour and do not forget the edges.*

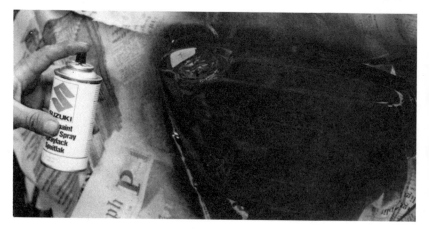

10d *When the second coat of colour is applied the tank will start to develop a gloss finish.*

Below:
11d *When the paint has completely dried, carefully remove the masking. The paint will still be 'soft' and sticky tape can pluck bits off.*

12d *Leave the paint to harden for a few days, then rub with a mildly abrasive polish followed by a good wax, to give a glass-like shine.*

13d Sometimes it is possible to avoid masking altogether. This tool box cover is first removed from the bike.

Below:
14d The captive bolt holding the knob can be released by sawing the washer halfway through (squeeze the edges together to use again).

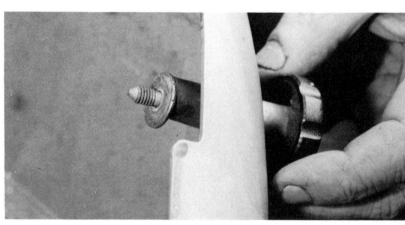

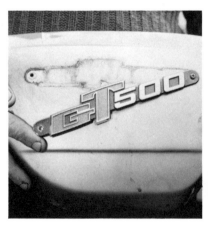

15d By undoing two phillips screws the lettering can be completely removed. Take care not to slip with the screwdriver . . .

16d The surface is then rubbed down with superfine emery paper until it is completely smooth. Deal with any damage in the usual way.

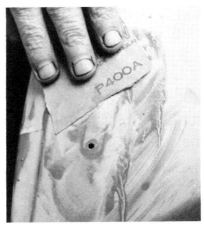

Below:
17d The cover is then thoroughly washed to remove any traces of rubbed down paint dust and, when dry, will be ready for spraying.

Above:
18d By supporting the cover in this way, the top, sides, and under edges are all accessible. Do not forget the newspaper underneath.

19d The cover is then sprayed with at least two coats each of primer and top coat. Remember to spray the bottom edges.

Spraying Mudguards
– series e

1e To save complicated masking the mudguard is removed. After the necessary repairs, it is thoroughly washed inside and out.

2e The easiest way to support a mudguard is to put an old aerosol can inside the nose of the mudguard but not touching the edges.

3e The primer is applied to the mudguard in two halves, but not in a definite line, to avoid ridges.

4e The top coat is also applied half a coat at a time but not two half coats at one end and then two at the other.

7 Lettering and Lining

Virtually all petrol tanks and many other items on a motor-cycle have lettering and lining on them to improve their appearance and to indicate the make and model. No matter how well a bike has been resprayed, without these markings its appearance suffers and it becomes difficult to sell. When the bike was originally made, the lines were either painted on by hand or put on by transfer. Re-lining by hand is an extremely tricky business and obtaining copies of the original manufacturer's transfers is either almost impossible or very expensive.

Lettering gives the same problems, with the exception of one or two early Yamahas and Suzukis which had their lettering made of metal on detachable plates.

If money is no problem, it is worth visiting a local motorcycle repair shop to get a quote for the lettering and lining. If it is, and the lettering is not in some exotic script and the lining is not very complex, there is no reason why you should not do it yourself.

For example, take the problem of painting a line on a petrol tank. With a pot of paint and a brush it is almost impossible to get a straight line, unless you are a signwriter, but stick two strips of masking tape about ⅛ inch apart and paint in the gap between them (it does not matter if the paint goes on the masking tape) and when the tape is removed, you have a clean straight ⅛ inch wide line. Stick one strip of masking tape level and the other so that the gap starts normally and then tapers to nothing and you will have a line tapering to a fine point. If the line is to end square, put another piece of tape over the gap at right angles. Remember that the shape of the gap between the tape determines the shape of the line.

When you come to the first bend you will discover that tape buckles when you try to make it go around a curve. To avoid this, use a piece of thin card or thick paper instead. Draw the required curve on the card and cut along the line. Apply an adhesive to the back of the two pieces of card (one that will not remove the paintwork) and stick them in place, leaving the appropriate gap between the two halves. This gap should match up with the gap between the masking tape so that a continuous line will be formed. The card will now fill the same purpose as the masking tape. When one line is dry, another may be formed next to it, making quite complex line groupings.

Whereas lines can be made with paint and masking tape, letters have to be bought. These are fairly easily obtainable from most D-I-Y shops in all sorts of shapes and sizes, but usually only in black and white. If these colours are suitable they are simply stuck in place and sprayed with clear lacquer to protect them from wear and tear.

However, if, for example, blue lettering was required on a red object, the object would first be sprayed blue. The white or black lettering would then be stuck lightly in place (NOT LACQUERED) and the object would then be resprayed red. As the letters act as a mask to the paintwork underneath them, when they are removed an exact copy of them will remain in blue and the rest of the object will, of course, be red.

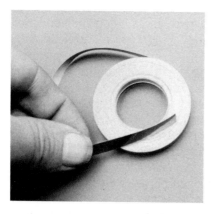

1 The simplest and quickest way to apply lines is to use stick-on lining. Called 'pin striping', these lines are obtainable from car accessory shops in a wide variety of colours and widths.

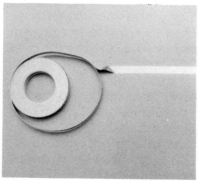

2 Make sure that the surface that the lining is to be applied to is clean and dry. Peel back the protective backing and stick the line firmly in place. If you make a mistake, you can simply peel it off again.

3 *The shape of the ends of the line depend on the angle that the lining is cut off. Rub the lining down with a cloth to make sure it sticks thoroughly. For extra protection it can be sprayed with clear varnish.*

4 *A paint line is simply made by sticking two pieces of masking tape parallel to each other. The gap between the pieces of tape will be the width of the line.*

Below:
5 *Two pieces of tape are then placed crosswise to form the ends of the line. The angle of these pieces of tape determine the shape of the ends of the line.*

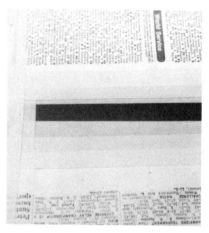

6 Newspapers and masking tape are then used to mask off the surrounding area, so that only the area forming the line can be sprayed. For thin lines, don't bother with this additional masking. Simply paint between the tape with a small brush.

7 Spray with a couple of coats of paint of the required colour. Wait until the paint has completely dried before carefully peeling back the masking tape.

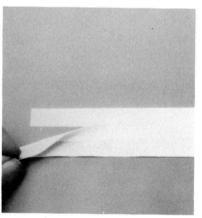

8 Allow the paint line to harden for a couple of days. Then rub down gently with a mildly abrasive polish to 'sharpen up' the edges.

Opposite top:
9 The paintwork on this Yamaha is easy to duplicate. Basically it consists of two thin lines, some adhesive black lettering and a thick broken line.

Opposite centre:
10 To produce this broken line effect, first mask to make a thick line. In this particular case the ends of the line are masked to produce a slight angle.

Opposite bottom:
11 Thin strips of masking tape are then cut and placed across the area forming the line, in a regular pattern. When the masking is removed after spraying, a broken line will be left.

12 Unless you are exceptionally talented, the only way you will have any success with lettering is to use the stick on type. Available in an impressive range of sizes and styles, but generally only in black and white.

13 If you only need black or white lettering, clean the area to be lettered thoroughly. Then remove the protective backing from the letters and stick them in place (they are self adhesive). A coating of clear varnish makes them last longer.

14 If you need a different colour, first spray the area to be lettered the required colour, and when dry stick the letters in place. These will act as a mask.

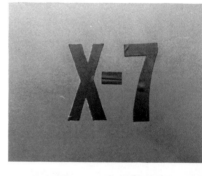

15 Then respray the whole area in the finished colour of the tank. The letters will almost disappear, but can be located by their raised edges.

16 *When the paint has thoroughly dried, use the edge of a sharp bladed knife (raid the kitchen,?) to lift the edge of the letters and peel them away carefully.*

17 *The stick on letters have formed a mask to the final colour and their exact shape will appear in the colour underneath. Wait a couple of days, then rub with a mildly abrasive polish to sharpen up the edges.*

18 *White lettering and gold lining produce this attractive design on a black tank. The masking for the lining should be thought out carefully and if possible tried out on a piece of card first.*

8 Personalizing with Paint

If you want to ride something 'different' and cannot afford to go out and buy a piece of hand-made exotic machinery, you can always change the appearance of a mass-produced bike. There are two ways of doing this – with paint and with accessories.

Paint is by far the cheapest way but it is fairly permanent and time consuming. The only bits and pieces needed are masking tape, a few pieces of card, a pair of scissors, a fairly fine paint brush, a few newspapers and of course the appropriate aerosols of spray paint.

First start with the aerosols of paint. Do not go to a motorcycle shop, go to a car accessory shop. They stock a larger range. Manufacturers like Holts and Spectra have large racks of spray paints, all in different shades and colours. Each aerosol has a sample of its contents sprayed on the lid, so in one visit you can choose your main colour and any others you need to complement it. Most shops will let you take the can tops out to your bike to see how the colours will look.

As well as the normal shades and colours, many shops stock metalflake paints. These have small pieces of metal flakes mixed in with the paint. These small pieces of metal glisten through the finished paintwork and if it is sprayed over with a few coats of clear varnish, it looks like a sheet of deep plate glass with metal floating in it.

Spectra have even produced a range of heat-resistant engine paints, so you can have a red, yellow, blue or even green engine if the mood so takes you. There is no reason why you should not use one of the range of hazard warning aerosols in Day-glow, but do not expect to sell your bike to a little old lady afterwards!

When deciding on a design the best way to go about it is to find out what effects are possible and whether you like them or not.

In the previous chapter, methods of producing lines were discussed, but what is not generally realised is that lines in 'reverse' can be most attractive. Cut out a strip of thin card, about ⅛ inch wide, lay it on an object and spray it with an aerosol. A negative line will be produced in the form of the original colour of the object. It will have a sharp border either side, made up of the colour of the spray, which gradually fades the further it gets from the line, until it blends into the original colour. Hold the strip of card ¼ inch or so away from the object when spraying and the edges of the line become blurred, giving a different effect.

You could, for example, spray around the two edges of a square of card and, depending on how far away it was held, produce a sharp or blurred chevron. Move the card along a little each time and any number of interesting repeat patterns can be produced; depending on the shape of the edge of the card.

A similar but slightly different effect can be obtained by cutting a hole or pattern in the centre of a piece of card and spraying through it as opposed to around it. A classical example of this is spraying through a piece of lace.

The best way to fully exploit these techniques, is to practise them singly and then variously in combinations until the desired effect is achieved. Practise on a piece of card or metal. Each time you want to try something different, spray over with primer and start again.

Never forget that personalising with paint is really spraying and the same basic rules apply as those discussed in the chapter on 'the technique of spraying'. Always spray on to a clean, grease-free surface, never spray to wet paint and always keep the aerosol moving or you will get paint runs. Finally if you are unhappy with the finished results, you can always rub the whole area down with superfine emery paper to get rid of any ridges caused by extra thicknesses of paint at the edges of patterns, etc, wash, prime and start again.

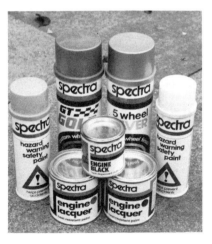

1 When looking at paints for customizing, it is worth considering the unusual. Day-glow hazard warning paints and different coloured engine lacquers are just a couple of ideas.

81

2 *If your design uses straight lines, do it the easy way with masking tape. The principle is the same as that used in lining.*

3 *This time be more adventurous with your shapes. Set the masking tape at strong angles and remember that the shape inside the tape is the shape of the finished colour panel.*

4 *Mask off the surrounding area with newspaper stuck to tape (as described in Chapter 7 Lettering and Lining) and spray with the required colour.*

5 *When the masking is removed, a sharp coloured shape is left. Allow the paint to harden for a few days and then gently blend it in with a mildly abrasive polish.*

6 *Complicated shapes can be made using this method, providing they can be broken down into straight lines. When tape meets on the inside edge of a design, make sure it doesn't overlap to give an odd shape.*

7 *It is often easier to cut the ends of both pieces of tape slightly short, then stick a separate piece of tape in place to give a tidy junction.*

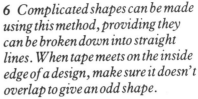

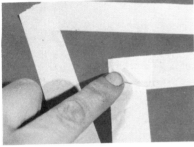

Below:
8 *Mask and spray in the usual way. Remove the masking tape and you are left with an interesting panel of colour suitable for the side of a tank.*

9 *It is not difficult to mask for two colours as long as a little common sense is used. If both sets of masking are done at the same time, it is easier to visualise the finished result.*

10 *Start by masking for the first colour. In this case it is intended to be a flash along the top edge and down the side of a tank.*

11 *Then mask for the second colour, which will be two bars of colour on the side of the tank. Make sure that there is always a gap between the two colours.*

12 *Using tape and paper, carefully mask off the area to receive the first colour and spray.*

13 Remove the tape and paper but not the tape forming the shape of the first area, as it may also form part of the shape of the second area.

14 Next using tape and paper, mask off the area to receive the second colour. Do not stick tape over the area just painted as it will still be soft and may pull off.

Below:
15 After spraying the second colour, carefully remove all the tape and your completed design will emerge. If you are not certain about your design or choice of colour, try it out on a practice piece before spraying the bike.

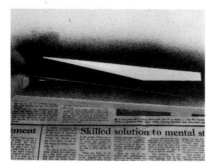

16 *Odd shaped solid objects, if laid flat and sprayed produce a sharp edge with the sprayed colour extending outwards with decreasing density.*

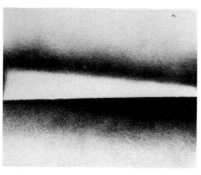

17 *If one edge is lifted away, the edge not in contact will give a softer line. The further the edge is away from the object being sprayed, the softer will be its outline.*

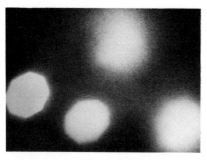

18 *Odd shaped holes can be cut in pieces of card and the spray directed through the holes onto the object. As can be seen, the nearer the hole is to the object, the sharper its outline appears.*

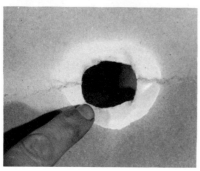

19 *Be careful when making patterns using this method as wet paint builds up on the edge of the hole and may drip onto the surface being sprayed. After every three or four sprays, wipe the edge of the hole.*

Above:
20 As an example of what can be achieved with patience and an eye for design, 'Tarmac Teaser' takes a lot of beating. Owned by Peter Stevens, President of the Custom Bike Club, it has won an impressive array of cups and trophys.

21 Manufacturers are now producing their own range of customized bikes. This Yamaha 750 U.S. Custom comes complete with raised handlebars, American style petrol tank and distinctive paint job.

9 Personalizing with Accessories

The easy way to change the appearance of a bike is to fit 'bolt-on' goodies. These range from farings, panniers and complex multi-pipe exhaust systems to clip on handlebars and footboards for pillion passengers. The only skills needed are the ability to fasten a couple of nuts and bolts together and fasten a few wires. You will also need money, and this or the lack of it will probably decide the extent to which this kind of personalising will be carried out.

It is generally agreed that the greatest change in appearance for the least amount of money is achieved by fitting a faring. Farings can be split into two types, handlebar and full.

A handlebar faring is attached to the handlebars and front forks and the cheapest kind costs about the same as a couple of tyres. The two extremes of style are cockpit and touring, with sports somewhere in between.

The cockpit faring is the smallest and, apart from keeping some of the wind and weather off the riders middle, its function is mainly cosmetic. Because of its small size and weight, it has very little effect on the bikes handling.

The touring style is the biggest and heaviest of the handlebar farings, its main purpose being to protect the riders upper body, arms and hands from the weather. Most extend from about the rider's eye level to well below the headlamp and are wider than the handlebars in order to protect the rider's hands.

Being rather heavy, they make the rider use more muscle power when riding through town traffic and as they are bulky and connected to the handlebars and forks, they can cause handling problems in high winds and at speed. To compensate for this, they give more weather protection. Fitting takes about half a day.

Full farings cost around three times as much as handlebar farings and take twice as long to fit. They are available in all sorts of shapes, sizes, and colours, from the ultra compact full racing faring to the remarkably bulky American style farings with built-in luggage compartments. Full farings represent the ultimate in head-to-toe weather protection and handling is not usually affected as the faring is fastened to the frame of the bike. They also present a bigger area to be seen by other road users and offer some protection to arms and legs in a tumble. Some farings are produced specifically for one model of bike, while others will fit a wide range of bikes, just by fitting different brackets. This is well worth remembering if you are in the habit of changing machines.

Another major area of bolt-on goodies are connected with carburation and exhaust. Large chrome carburettor bell mouths and exotic exhaust systems may look good but they can cause problems. Whip the air filter assembly off a two-stroke and replace it with a wire-covered bell mouth, without having the carburettor re-jetted and the engine will run weak, resulting in horribly expensive things like seized engines, melted pistons, etc.

1 Handlebar farings are fairly cheap, easy to fit, and make a great deal of difference to a bike's appearance. This 'Harrier' faring comes ready custom striped, has a tinted windscreen and costs about the same as a couple of tyres.

89

Exhaust systems, especially those sold on claims of increased performance, can often alter the characteristics of an engine. For the sake of an extra mile an hour or so the bottom end performance could suffer. If in doubt, consult the manufacturers of the items you are thinking of buying and you could cross-check with the importers of your bike. Bearing these points in mind, nothing really tops off a customised bike like a really beautiful exhaust system.

2 For around twice as much, this full faring gives head to toe protection from the elements and a certain amount of leg protection in a tumble. Its plain white surface gives lots of scope for the custom paint enthusiast.

3 If you are feeling rich and have a bike big enough to take the bulk, this American style faring is probably the ultimate. It has its own built in side lights and indicators and boasts its own lockable glove box and map pockets.

4 *Any money left? Then try this matching American style top box and pannier set. Robust and beautifully made, you can startle people behind with the impressive array of ultra-bright built-in stop lights.*

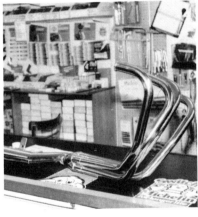

5 *Special exhaust pipes do look impressive. Make sure from the manufacturers that they meet the relevant noise emission laws or something in blue will grab you at the traffic lights!*

6 *Additional lighting comes in handy in the winter months. Available in different shapes and sizes, a smart set of lights can look good, but don't overdo it. The penalty is a flat battery.*

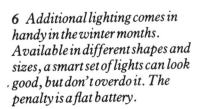

10 Prevention

Having at last got the bike looking good, it is important to keep it that way. Wash it regularly with lots of soapy water and do not polish it unless it is absolutely clean, because little bits of dirt and grit on the surface will act as an abrasive and scratch the paintwork.

A nylon (not metal) pan scourer is ideal for removing mild rust from odd shaped chrome areas like wheel rims and rear suspension coil springs. Tackle any scratched or chipped paintwork as soon as it occurs. Do not wait for it to go rusty. As a temporary measure, an aerosol can be sprayed into its own lid for a couple of seconds and the paint in the lid used to touch up any chips. If a brush is not handy, a drip on the end of a matchstick will hold back the rust for a week or so, until there is time to do the job properly.

Where rust starts in a place which is difficult to reach, use a non-acidic rust remover to avoid the danger of insufficient flushing and subsequent acid damage to adjacent parts.

Finally, avoid needless damage. Do not put anything on the tank that might scratch it (crash helmets have sharp buckles). Do not let buckles on clothing catch the bike as you get on and off and do not take the petrol filler cap on and off with gloves on. A few months of this and a ring of scratches will appear on the tank.

1 Avoid unnecessary damage. These scratches were caused by constantly removing a screw petrol filler cap with gloves on. Loose belt buckles can also scratch the tank.

2 *The best way to protect a bike against the elements is with a good coating of wax or silicone polish. Wash thoroughly first or grit will get trapped in the polishing cloth and scratch the paintwork.*

3 *Chrome needs protecting too. Either use a chrome cleaner that leaves a protective coating of wax or silicones, or wax separately after using the chrome polish.*

4 *Do not let dirt and mud build up on the engine fins, or they won't dissipate the heat efficiently and you could get overheating problems. Clean with a long nylon bristled (not metal) brush.*

5 Pit marks of corrosion on the engine are caused by the layer of protective clear lacquer breaking down. Before it gets too bad, repolish with a metal polish and protect with a clear spray-on lacquer.

6 If a bike is left standing for any length of time, water collects at the bottom of the wheel rims and causes rusting. The easiest way to remove this is with a nylon (not metal) pan scrubber.

7 This particular make of silencer forms a water trap with its holding bracket. Give areas like this particular attention when cleaning or rust will get a hold and eventually eat through the silencer.

8 When carrying out repairs, always use the correct sized spanners on plated nuts. Use of the wrong sized spanner on this nut has caused the plating to split and consequently rusting.

94

9 *Just because an item is made of aluminium, don't think that chipped paintwork can be ignored. This aluminium headstock hasn't rusted, it has corroded instead! Use superfine emery paper to remove corrosion and then re-paint.*

10 *When removing rust from areas which receive heavy physical scuffing, such as footrest brackets, try using an organic rust remover. When dry these products leave a tough flexible skin which protects against future rusting.*

11 *There is also a safety aspect to regular cleaning. It was noticed that this mudguard had rotted from underneath its fixing bracket. If left, it would have eventually wrapped itself around the wheel, causing a nasty accident.*

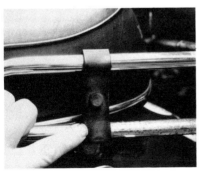

12 *Don't forget the accessories. While the chrome on rear carriers seems to survive quite well, the galvanised brackets rust at the slightest provocation. Painting them black or silver when new saves a lot of trouble.*

95

Acknowledgements

The Author gratefully acknowledges the assistance given by the following,

Nick Harvey of The Institute of Motorcycling.
Spectra Automotive Products.
Garry Taylor of Brandmark International.
Holt Lloyd Ltd.
Melton Products Ltd.
Peter Stevens of the Custom Bike Club.